Global Issues

Sustainable Cities

Cheryl Jakab

Smart Apple Media

This edition first published in 2010 in the United States of America by Smart Apple Media.
All rights reserved. No part of this book may be reproduced in any form or by any means without
written permission from the publisher.

Smart Apple Media
P.O. Box 3263
Mankato, MN 56002

First published in 2009 by
MACMILLAN EDUCATION AUSTRALIA PTY LTD
15–19 Claremont Street, South Yarra, Australia 3141

Visit our Web site at www.macmillan.com.au or go directly to www.macmillanlibrary.com.au

Associated companies and representatives throughout the world.

Copyright © Cheryl Jakab 2009

Library of Congress Cataloging-in-Publication Data

Jakab, Cheryl.
    Sustainable cities / Cheryl Jakab.
       p. cm. – (Global issues)
    Includes index.
    ISBN 978-1-59920-454-3 (hardcover)
    1. Urban ecology (Sociology)–Juvenile literature. 2. City planning–Environmental aspects–Juvenile literature. 3.
    Urbanization–Juvenile literature. 4. Sustainable development–Juvenile literature. I. Title.
    HT241.J36 2010
    307.76–dc22
                            2009002023

Edited by Julia Carlomagno
Text and cover design by Cristina Neri, Canary Graphic Design
Page layout by Christine Deering and Domenic Lauricella
Photo research by Jes Senbergs

Printed in the United States

Acknowledgments
The author and the publisher are grateful to the following for permission to reproduce copyright material:

Front cover photograph: People on bicycles at rush hour, Beijing, China, photo by Nicholas Pavloff/Getty Images

Photos courtesy of: © Arup. Artist's impression of Dongtan eco-city, designed by Arup, 27; © Nazira/Dreamstime.
com, 16; DW Stock Picture Library, 20; Getty Images, 26; AFP/Getty Images, 6 (right), 7 (bottom), 9, 10, 13, 19;
Justin Guariglia/Getty Images, 7 (top), 25; Hisham Ibrahim/Getty Images, 11; Yann Layma/Getty Images, 24; ©
George Clerk/Istockphoto, 8; © Daniel Halvorson/Istockphoto, 5; © Noel Voloh/Istockphoto, 18; CH2 image
courtesy of City of Melbourne, 23; Jodi Cobb/National Geographic Image Collection, 7 (middle), 17; Photolibrary/
© Andrew Butterton/Alamy, 22; Photolibrary/ © Cameron Davidson/Alamy, 6 (left), 21; Photolibrary/ © Stan
Kujawa/Alamy, 15; Photolibrary/ © Melvyn Longhurst/Alamy, 12; Photolibrary/ © Frances M Roberts/Alamy, 29;
Tim Wessbecher, 14.

While every care has been taken to trace and acknowledge copyright, the publisher tenders their apologies for any
accidental infringement where copyright has proved untraceable. Where the attempt has been unsuccessful, the
publisher welcomes information that would redress the situation.

Please note
At the time of printing, the Internet addresses appearing in this book were correct. Owing to the dynamic nature of
the Internet, however, we cannot guarantee that all these addresses will remain correct.

Contents

Glossary Words
When a word is printed in **bold**, you can look up its meaning in the Glossary on page 31.

Facing Global Issues

Hi there! This is Earth speaking. Will you spare a moment to listen to me? I have some very important things to discuss.

We must face up to some urgent environmental problems! All living things depend on my environment, but the way you humans are living at the moment, I will not be able to keep looking after you.

The issues I am worried about are:

- the effects of **global warming**
- the health of natural environments
- the use of **nonrenewable** energy supplies
- the environmental impact of unsustainable cities
- the build-up of toxic waste in the environment
- a reliable water supply for all

My global challenge to you is to find a sustainable way of living. Read on to find out what people around the world are doing to try to help.

Fast Fact
Sustainable development is a form of growth that lets us meet our present needs while leaving resources for future generations to meet their needs too.

What's the Issue?
Unsustainable Cities

More than half of Earth's population lives in towns and cities. Today, many cities use **unsustainable** amounts of **natural resources**. As more people move to **urban areas**, these cities will not be able to provide for them. How to make cities sustainable is an urgent issue that we must tackle today.

Urban Habitats

Cities can be thought of as urban habitats, or places where people live, eat and work. Like natural habitats, urban habitats must meet the needs of their **inhabitants**. The needs of people living in urban habitats include access to:

- fresh water, food, and shelter
- reliable energy supplies
- efficient transportation and waste removal services
- opportunities for work and recreation

Today, some urban inhabitants have all of their needs met, while the needs of others are not met at all.

Fast Fact
For the first time in history, most of Earth's population lives in towns and cities. In 2008, more than 3.3 billion people were living in cities.

Sustainable Cities

Sustainable cities can provide for the needs of their inhabitants and minimize their impacts on the environment. However, many of today's cities have large numbers of people who do not have homes or jobs. Most cities also use unsustainable amounts of natural resources, such as energy, water, and food. People need to learn how to make cities sustainable so that everyone, today and in the future, can have their needs met.

Large, crowded cities often cannot meet the needs of all their inhabitants.

Issues with Unsustainable

Issues with unsustainable cities around the globe include:
- lack of housing and resources due to unplanned urban growth (see issue 1)
- unequal access to resources (see issue 2)
- **traffic congestion** and other transportation problems (see issue 3)
- damage to the environment and wasted resources due to **inefficient** buildings (see issue 4)
- growing urban populations in many cities (see issue 5)

N O R T H

A M E R I C A

United States

N O R T H

A T L A N T I C

O C E A N

S O

A T L

O C

ISSUE 4

United States
Cities are growing as more people build houses on land around cities. See pages 20–23.

Fast Fact
Cities are responsible for 75 percent of the world's energy consumption and 80 percent of greenhouse gas emissions.

ISSUE 1

Gaborone, Botswana
Many people live in temporary housing due to a lack of **urban planning**. See pages 8–11.

Cities Around the Globe

ISSUE 5
Chongqing, China
The population is growing too fast for adequate services to be provided. See pages 24–27.

ISSUE 3
Bangkok, Thailand
Traffic congestion is causing transportation and health problems. See pages 16–19.

ISSUE 2
Mumbai, India
Some people live in luxury apartments while others live in slums. See pages 12–15.

ASIA

Chongqing

Mumbai

Bangkok

AFRICA

INDIAN

Gaborone

OCEAN

TH

TIC

AN

A

Unplanned Growth

As urban populations grow, more houses are built on the edges of cities. However, much of this growth is not planned. Often, many houses are crammed onto small areas of land.

Growing Urban Populations

Each year, urban populations grow as people move from **rural** areas to cities. As modern technologies develop, there is less work available on farms and more work available in industries in urban areas. This is why large numbers of people moved into urban areas during the 1800s and 1900s, particularly in the western world. These countries are now known as **developed countries**. Similar changes are occurring in **developing countries** today.

Lack of Housing

Many urban populations are growing so rapidly that many people cannot find houses to live in. Large, unplanned **squatter settlements** have developed on the edges of many large cities, particularly in Asia and Africa. Many residents are forced to live in **informal housing** as areas become overcrowded. These areas often have little access to energy supplies and transportation.

Fast Fact
There are now more people living in urban areas in Africa than there are in North America. Many of these people live in squatter settlements or informal housing.

Many people who move to urban areas live in informal housing on the edges of cities.

Many people on the outskirts of Gaborone live in unplanned settlements.

CASE STUDY

Unplanned Growth in Gaborone

Gaborone, the capital of Botswana, in Africa, has a growing population. The city is facing **urban sprawl**, high levels of **unemployment**, and poverty.

Land for Housing

To house its growing population, the city of Gaborone provides people with plots of land to build houses. These plots belong to the local government and people pay rent for them. Houses built on these plots belong to the homeowners for 99 years. While this approach has helped many people to find housing, it has created large, sprawling suburbs that take up huge amounts of land.

ISSUE 1

Gaborone's Projected Population Growth

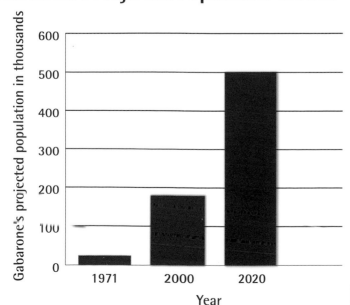

Gaborone's projected population in thousands

- 600
- 500
- 400
- 300
- 200
- 100
- 0

Year: 1971, 2000, 2020

Unplanned Settlements

Many of the poorest people in Gaborone cannot afford to rent plots of land. They live in unplanned settlements on the edges of the city. Many of these settlements have poor waste removal services. Stormwater channels often fill with mud, sand, and garbage. When these channels overflow, they can spread diseases.

Gaborone's population is predicted to grow to 500,000 by 2020.

9

Toward a Sustainable Future: Urban Planning

Urban planning is the process by which governments and city planners map out new housing and services. Information about growing populations can be collected to help with urban planning.

Collecting Information

Collecting information about cities can help governments plan for the future. Many local governments in developing countries have little knowledge about the state of their cities. They need up-to-date data to find out what their problems are. Organizations can collect many types of information about cities, including:

- rates of population growth
- numbers of houses, apartments, and informal houses
- amounts of water and energy supplies used
- numbers of people using **public facilities**, such as roads

The United Nations State of the World's Cities Report 2006/7 was the first report to collect information on the state of cities worldwide. It shows that cities and towns are using unsustainable amounts of resources, such as water and energy.

Planning for the Future

When governments have information about the problems in their cities, they can plan for the future. Urban planning can help to ensure that all people have access to better transportation, housing, energy supplies and fresh drinking water. Good planning can reduce problems of unemployment and poverty.

Urban planning in the city of Brasilia helps to ensure that enough roads are built close to city centers.

The Alexandria Development Project is building roads to allow more of Alexandria's residents to access services and facilities.

CASE STUDY
Urban Planning in Alexandria

The Alexandria Development Project in Egypt is an example of good urban planning. The project supports local development, provides services to the poor, and reduces pollution in **industrial areas**.

Access to Services

Alexandria is Egypt's second-largest city and its population has increased by three million in the last 50 years. People are moving from rural areas to the edges of Alexandria, where there is little access to the city's services and facilities, such as public hospitals and schools. However, most people who live in the city center have access to these services.

Plans to Supply Services

The Alexandria Development Project plans to provide access to services for many people living in informal housing on the city's fringes. Nearly half of the funds for the project will be spent on roads, so that people in isolated areas can gain access to the city's facilities. The rest of the money will be spent on ensuring that water supplies are reliable and on protecting the city from floods.

Population Growth in Alexandria	
Year	Population
1960	1,500,000
1966	1,800,000
1976	2,300,000
1986	2,900,000
2007	3,750,000
2008	3,800,000

Unequal Access to Resources

In cities across the globe, there is unequal access to housing, transportation, and education. Many of the richest people **consume** more than their share of resources and live in luxury, while people with little money often live in informal housing.

Unequal Access

In many cities today, there is a large divide between the rich and the poor. Some people live in luxury apartments, while others live in informal housing. Some people use large amounts of water and energy to run their homes, while others have little or no access to energy supplies.

Living in Luxury

Fast Fact
In 2008, the world's most expensive apartments were built. These apartments overlook Hyde Park in London, and each apartment costs about $188 million.

Living in luxury in a city where others live in poverty is sometimes called living "off-world." Off-world houses have been described as fantasy theme parks because they are so different to other houses around them. Off-world luxury housing is most often found in cities where the very poorest people live, such as Buenos Aires, Cairo, Jakarta, Dubai, and Mumbai.

Living in luxury can have consequences for the environment. Large houses take up large amounts of land and need lots of water and energy to run. In many of the world's largest cities today, these resources are being used at unsustainable rates.

One luxury house in Dubai may be bigger than the whole neighborhood of informal housing surrounding it.

CASE STUDY

Luxury Apartments and Slums in Mumbai

ISSUE 2

Luxury apartments are being built above slums in Mumbai, India. These homes cost millions of dollars, while people living in the slums below try to survive on very little.

Luxury Apartments

Luxury apartments in Mumbai often have many special features, such as marble floors, rooftop gardens and spas. They may also have features such as:

- elevators
- cinemas
- sports fields
- banquet halls
- fingerprint identification systems

In the next few years, more of these luxury apartments will be built. People who live in these apartments include bankers, IT experts, and other businesspeople who have recently become wealthy due to the growth of India's economy. Currently, demand for luxury apartments is greater than supply.

Slums

Below many of these luxury apartments, millions of people live in slums and informal housing. It is estimated that around 84,000 new homes are needed in Mumbai each year, although only around 55,000 are built. Today, nearly 10 million people live in Mumbai's slums, many without access to running water.

In Mumbai, blocks of luxury apartments tower over large slums.

13

Toward a Sustainable Future: Using Fewer Resources

If people use fewer resources, there are more resources to be shared with others. Using fewer resources also helps to make cities more sustainable and reduces the impact on the environment.

Smaller Houses

Well-designed, smaller houses can reduce the environmental impacts of each household, while still being comfortable places to live. Smaller houses use fewer materials in their construction, take up less space and use less energy to heat and cool.

Compact Cities

Compact cities are spread over the smallest possible areas. They have smaller houses and apartments in high-rise buildings. In compact cities everyone is closer to all services, so the distances people need to travel are reduced. Making cities compact may be the best way to limit resource use and make cities more sustainable in the future.

Fast Fact

The average size of a new home in Europe is around 1,130 square feet (105 sq m), compared to around 2,411 square feet (224 sq m) in the United States.

Some modern houses in Europe are compact so that they only use small amounts of land.

This ecovillage in Wallington, the United Kingdom, uses solar panels and wind turbines to generate energy.

CASE STUDY
Ecovillages

Ecovillages can minimize impacts on the environment. They can also offer ideas for how to create sustainable cities, in which everyone has access to resources.

What is an Ecovillage?

An ecovillage is an urban or rural community of people who live in small social groups and explore low-impact ways of living. Ecovillages are designed to protect the well-being of people and the environment. People combine ideas about growing plants and food, sustainable buildings, green technologies, and alternative energy sources to minimize their impacts on the environment, now and in the future.

Ideas for Compact Cities

While ecovillages are often small, the ideas they apply may be useful in creating sustainable compact cities. The Global Ecovillage Network shares the practical ideas, information, and technologies that people learn through living in ecovillages.

Fast Fact
In 1998, the United Nations listed ecovillages among the Top 100 Listing of Best Practices for sustainable living.

15

Transportation Problems

Many of the world's largest cities are suffering from problems with transportation. More people are using cars and public transportation systems are becoming crowded and unreliable.

Increase in Cars

The number of cars using roads in cities and towns increases daily. Traffic causes congestion, air pollution, car crashes, and noise. As the number of cars on roads increases, these problems will also increase.

People are also traveling further in their cars. As towns and cities grew, cars became an important form of transportation for many people. Freeways were built in order to avoid traffic congestion in towns and cities. City planners did not realize that, as more freeways were built, people would use their cars more.

Public Transportation

In many places where the use of cars increased, public transportation services declined. Many cities had public transportation networks in the late 1800s and early 1900s. These networks served the public well before the era of cars and freeways. In many cities today, the growth in population has not been matched with an increase in public transportation services.

Traffic congestion is a major problem in many cities today.

Fast Fact
In California, the use of cars doubled between 1970 and 1990. It grew more than four times faster than the population.

Some people in Bangkok, Thailand, spend hours each day stuck in traffic.

CASE STUDY
Traffic Congestion in Bangkok

Thailand's capital, Bangkok, has some of the worst traffic congestion in the world. More cars are being added to the roads each day and pollution from traffic is causing health problems.

Health Problems

There are few regulations in Bangkok to control air pollution from traffic. The pollution from car exhausts is making people ill. Dense clouds of exhaust fumes are causing people to develop coughs and breathing problems. Nearly one in six **outpatients** in Bangkok hospitals suffer from breathing problems.

More Cars

Today, there are more cars on Bangkok's roads than ever before. As the economy grows, the population is getting wealthier and many people who could not afford cars in the past are now buying them. **Gridlock** is such a big problem that police officers often deliver babies and doctors drive out from hospitals in motorcycle taxis to help patients.

Toward a Sustainable Future: Integrated Transportation Systems

Integrated transportation systems ensure that all forms of transportation work together so that people can move around their cities with ease. Integrated transportation systems can reduce energy use and air pollution.

Public Transportation

People can use public transportation to reduce their reliance on cars. Effective public transportation systems can move people and goods around cities quickly and efficiently. If more people catch buses or trains instead of drive cars, then the amount of air pollution and traffic congestion in cities will also be reduced. In some cities, public transportation is at the center of integrated transportation systems.

Fast Fact

The Australian government estimates that if all the people who catch trains to work in Sydney, Australia, were to drive instead, the city would need at least 1,927 acres (780 ha) of extra parking lots.

Alternatives to Cars

People can also use other forms of transportation as alternatives to cars. Some cities promote cycling as part of their integrated transportation systems. In Copenhagen, Denmark, 30 to 40 percent of people ride bicycles to work. This reduces the amount of traffic on the roads and reduces air pollution in the city.

Many forms of transportation can be used in an integrated transportation system, including ferries.

The freeways were so empty during the Colombian city of Bogotá's eighth car-free day that people used the roads to play soccer.

CASE STUDY

Car-free Zones

Car-free zones and car-free days are being introduced in many cities across the world. These measures help to reduce people's reliance on cars and focus public attention on alternative forms of transportation.

Car-free Zones

Car-free zones have reduced car use in many cities. By 2007, more than 60 European cities had declared their city centers car-free. In Athens, each car can only be used every second day because of pollution problems. License plates ending in an odd number are allowed to enter the city one day, and plates ending in an even number the next. In London, drivers must pay to enter the city center. Similar measures are being put in place in Central and South America.

Car-free Days

Many countries now have car-free days in order to encourage people to use other forms of transportation. These days highlight the need for alternative means of transportation and show that the public supports measures to reduce car use. Approximately 75 percent of the population takes part in Britain's car-free day each year.

Fast Fact

Campaigns by members of the United Kingdom's anti-road movement have stopped the construction of many new roads and freeways.

Environmental Impacts of Building

Throughout the 1900s, little thought was given to the environmental impacts of building homes and city structures. Today, many buildings use large amounts of resources and cause damage to the environment.

Design of Buildings

The design of many buildings in cities across the world causes unsustainable amounts of resources to be used. Most of these buildings:

- are made from materials that are taken from unsustainable sources
- rely on heaters and air conditioners to control temperatures
- use artificial lighting and insulation

Location of Buildings

Some city buildings take up large areas of land, so that many cities sprawl over long distances. Most cities are also surrounded by suburbs that are filled with houses on large blocks of land. As more people build large houses on new land, more roads and facilities must be built to service these people. This causes damage to the environment and destroys the natural habitats of local wildlife.

Many city skyscrapers use energy inefficiently, particularly because people leave lights on at night.

Residents in this ex-urban development in Utah rely on their cars as there is little public transportation nearby.

CASE STUDY

Ex-urban Developments in the United States

Ex-urban housing developments are small groups of houses built further away from cities than most suburbs. More ex-urban developments are being created as land near cities is built up or becomes expensive.

Advantages of Ex-urban Developments

There are many advantages to living in ex-urban housing developments. Most of these developments are surrounded by nature. They are often too far away from city centers to suffer from air pollution from cars or industries. Also, houses in ex-urban developments are often cheaper than houses closer to city centers.

Disadvantages of Ex-urban Developments

There are also many disadvantages to living so far away from city centers. There is often only limited access to transportation and facilities for those living in distant suburbs. Roads are often built so that people in ex-urban developments can drive their cars into cities to access services. Building these roads and houses causes damage to the environment and destroys the natural habitats of local wildlife.

Fast Fact
Many houses in ex-urban developments are very large. The size of the average American house has more than doubled since the 1950s.

Toward a Sustainable Future: Green Buildings

Green buildings are designed to be energy-efficient and to minimize impacts on the environment. Green buildings are starting to be built in cities all around the world.

Designing and Constructing Green Buildings

Designing and constructing green buildings can help to make cities more sustainable into the future. It is estimated that nearly half of the buildings needed to house the world's population in 2030 do not yet exist. This means that there will be many opportunities for city planners to build green buildings in the future.

Features of Green Buildings

Green buildings are designed with many energy-efficient features, including:

- **passive solar** heating and cooling
- energy-efficient lighting
- high-quality insulation
- natural ventilation
- power sourced from renewable energy sources

Many green buildings also use plants to help with natural heating and cooling. Research shows that buildings with plants on the outside are cooler in the summer and warmer in the winter. In the future, many green buildings may actually look green, due to the green plants that cover them.

Fast Fact
An average-sized home with insulation uses far less energy for heating and cooling than a home twice its size with high-quality insulation.

These green buildings are part of a sustainable housing exhibition in Watford, the United Kingdom.

CASE STUDY
Melbourne's Council House Two

In 2006, the first green office building opened in Melbourne, Australia. Council House Two (CH2) has many green features to reduce its impacts on the environment.

Features of CH2

CH2 has many green features, including:

- natural lighting
- natural ventilation
- recycled timber shutters for shade
- water-efficient taps and showerheads
- a wall of green plants to regulate temperatures

Green Technologies

Most of the green technology used in CH2 is not new. However, these green technologies have never been used together in one building before. As a result of energy-efficient green technologies, CH2 consumes only 15 percent of the energy that most buildings consume. As a result of water-efficient green technologies, CH2 uses about 30 percent of the water that an average building uses.

CH2 uses many green technologies, such as solar energy, wind power, and natural ventilation.

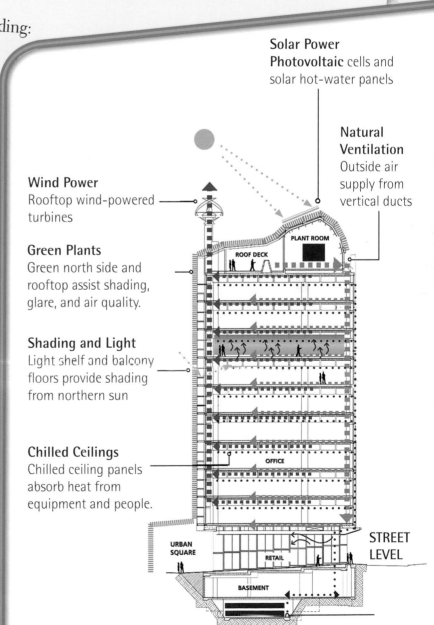

Solar Power
Photovoltaic cells and solar hot-water panels

Natural Ventilation
Outside air supply from vertical ducts

Wind Power
Rooftop wind-powered turbines

Green Plants
Green north side and rooftop assist shading, glare, and air quality.

Shading and Light
Light shelf and balcony floors provide shading from northern sun

Chilled Ceilings
Chilled ceiling panels absorb heat from equipment and people.

PLANT ROOM
ROOF DECK
OFFICE
URBAN SQUARE
RETAIL
STREET LEVEL
BASEMENT

The Rush to Cities

Today, millions of people are moving from rural areas to urban areas each year. Already, many cities cannot provide resources and services for their populations.

Unsustainable Resource Use

People in cities are using unsustainable amounts of resources. People in cities are:

- consuming too many resources too quickly
- wasting resources such as water and energy
- polluting the environment by using cars too often
- building inefficient buildings that use large amounts of land and resources

Inadequate Services

As urban populations grow, cities cannot provide services to all the people who live in them. Already, most cities must bring in food and water from other places to provide for their populations. Many waste removal systems and transportation systems are running at **capacity**. These systems will not be able to cope in the future as urban populations continue to grow. In cities with rapid population growth, many of these problems are already reaching crisis point.

Fast Fact

It is estimated that Earth's urban populations are growing by 180,000 people daily. In China an estimated 8.5 million people move to cities every year.

Some cities in China are growing so rapidly that city streets are becoming very crowded.

Chongqing suffers from poor air quality due to pollution.

CASE STUDY
Chongqing, the Fastest Growing City

In 2007, the United Nations' The State of the World's Cities Report named Chongqing, China, as the fastest growing city in the world. Chongqing is currently home to approximately 12 million people. In the next 10 years, Chongqing's population is expected to rise by four million.

A Growing Population

The population of Chongqing is growing rapidly as the Chinese government encourages people in rural areas to move to urban areas. China's industries are expanding, so more workers are needed in cities each year. China has many cities with more than 10 million people; these are called megacities. In 1978, only 18 percent of Chinese lived in cities, but by 2010 it is estimated that this figure will have risen to 50 percent.

Problems with Services and Air Pollution

Chongqing is growing so rapidly that services cannot be provided for people living in the city. There are problems with providing reliable waste removal services and, because the population is growing faster than Chongqing's industries, there are no longer enough jobs.

Chongqing also has problems with air pollution. Chongqing's biggest industries are steel production and motorbike and car manufacturing. Most of these industries are based in the city center and air pollution often spreads out across the city. Most days the city is covered in a thick cloud of smog.

Fast Fact
By 2030, it is predicted that the number of people living in cities around the world will have grown to almost 5 billion.

Toward a Sustainable Future: Ecocities

Countries around the world could work toward planning and building ecocities. Ecocities use resources efficiently and reduce environmental impacts.

What is an Ecocity?

An ecocity is a city that will be sustainable into the future because it minimizes impacts on the environment. The term "ecocity" is short for "ecologically sustainable city." In China, trial ecocities are being built. There are already plans to build at least 400 new ecocities in the next 20 years if the trials are successful.

Reducing Environmental Impacts

Ecocities aim to reduce their impacts on the environment by:

- using small amounts of land to house large numbers of people
- using resources efficiently by building green buildings and homes
- conserving resources by using green technologies such as water recycling and renewable energy

As Earth's population continues to grow, ecocities will be vital for a sustainable future. This is particularly the case in many parts of Asia, where large numbers of people are moving to urban areas.

In the future, large, sprawling cities may have more green buildings and trees, as ecocities will.

Plans for Dongtan show the environmental features of China's first ecocity, such as solar panels and green plants.

CASE STUDY
Dongtan Ecocity

Dongtan, China, has been planned as a demonstration ecocity. It will provide other countries with a model for how to develop ecocities.

Housing Urban Populations

Dongtan ecocity will provide a home for many thousands of people. The city will be located on Chongming Island in the Yangtze River Delta, about an hour's ferry ride from Shanghai. By 2010, Dongtan could house approximately 5,000 people and by 2050 it could house almost 500,000 people.

Using Resources Efficiently

Dongtan ecocity will use resources efficiently to minimize its impacts on the environment. The city is designed to be "beautiful and truly sustainable with a minimal **ecological footprint**." Dongtan will:

- recycle water and waste
- use energy from renewable sources
- ban cars that release pollution from the city center

ISSUE 5

27

What Can You Do? Help Your Community Become Sustainable

You can make suggestions about how to help your community become sustainable. You can also make your household more sustainable.

Take Action in Your Community

You can suggest ways to use fewer resources, or use resources more efficiently. Follow the steps below to take action in your community.

Action Plan

1. Find out whether your community has any of the following:
   - green buildings, or buildings that use some green technologies
   - reliable transportation and waste-disposal services
   - programs to recycle household garbage
   - a range of facilities, such as hospitals, roads, parks, and public libraries

2. Record three things that could improve your community, such as a car-free day, buildings that use green technologies, or a car-pooling program.

3. Choose one idea and write a letter to your local council or school asking them to consider your idea.

Make Your Household Sustainable

You can make your household more sustainable and contribute to a more sustainable community by using resources more efficiently. The table below lists some sustainability aims and ways that you could achieve them.

Sustainability Aim	This Can Be Achieved By
Reduce energy use	• switching off lights and electrical items at the power source • replacing standard light bulbs with energy-efficient light bulbs • encouraging your family to buy power from a green energy provider
Use less water	• taking shorter showers • using water from showers and baths to water gardens or wash cars • encouraging your family to buy a rainwater tank for your house
Reduce waste	• recycling plastic, metal, paper, and glass where possible • putting food waste in a compost bin to be used as fertiliser • wearing clothing handed down from your brothers and sisters
Reduce carbon emissions	• riding your bicycle or walking instead of being driven • using public transportation, such as trains and buses, where possible • sharing car rides with friends where possible

Buying locally grown produce reduces the amount of gasoline used to transport food, which helps to make your community more sustainable.

Toward a Sustainable Future

Well, I hope you now see that if you take up my challenge your world will be a better place. There are many ways to work toward a sustainable future. Imagine it ... a world with:

- decreasing rates of global warming
- protected ecosystems for all living things
- renewable fuel for most forms of transportation
- sustainable city development
- low risks of exposure to toxic substances
- a safe and reliable water supply for all

This is what you can achieve if you work together with my natural systems.

We must work together to live sustainably. That will mean a better environment and a better life for all living things on Earth, now and in the future.

Web Sites

For further information on sustainable cities, visit these websites:
- United Nations Population Fund State of World Population 2007
  www.unfpa.org/swp/2007/english/chapter_5/index.html
- World Health Organization Healthy Cities programme
  www.euro.who.int/healthy-cities
- Kids Corner Bike Quiz www.llysworney.com/html/kids_corner.html

Glossary

capacity
maximum levels

consume
use up

developed countries
countries with industrial development, a strong economy, and a high standard of living

developing countries
countries with less developed industry and a lower standard of living

ecological footprint
a measure of how much impact an activity has on the environment

global warming
a rise in average temperatures on Earth

gridlock
extreme traffic congestion, which occurs when roads are so blocked with traffic that cars do not move or move very slowly

industrial areas
parts of cities where industries are concentrated

inefficient
not done in the easiest way or by using the minimum amount of resources

informal housing
unplanned or unofficial housing settlements, in which housing does not conform to planning rules

inhabitants
people who live in a particular area

natural resources
materials people take from the earth to make products

nonrenewable
a resource that is limited in supply and cannot be replaced once it runs out

outpatients
people who are treated at hospitals for health problems, but do not need to be admitted

passive solar
technologies that use the sun to heat and cool buildings directly

photovoltaic
a device that is used to convert solar energy into electricity

public facilities
buildings or systems created to serve particular functions, such as roads or hospitals

rural
areas far away from cities, with low populations

slums
urban areas with poor living conditions

squatter settlements
communities of people who set up homes without permission on land they do not own

traffic congestion
too many cars on the road leading to overcrowding

unsustainable
a way of living that uses up natural resources very quickly

urban areas
areas with large human populations, such as big towns or cities

urban planning
organizing how towns and cities will look and how the needs of the residents will be provide

urban sprawl
the unplanned spreading of urban areas into new areas

unemployment
not having a job; not being employed

Index